RUBANK EDUCATIONAL LIBRARY No. 96

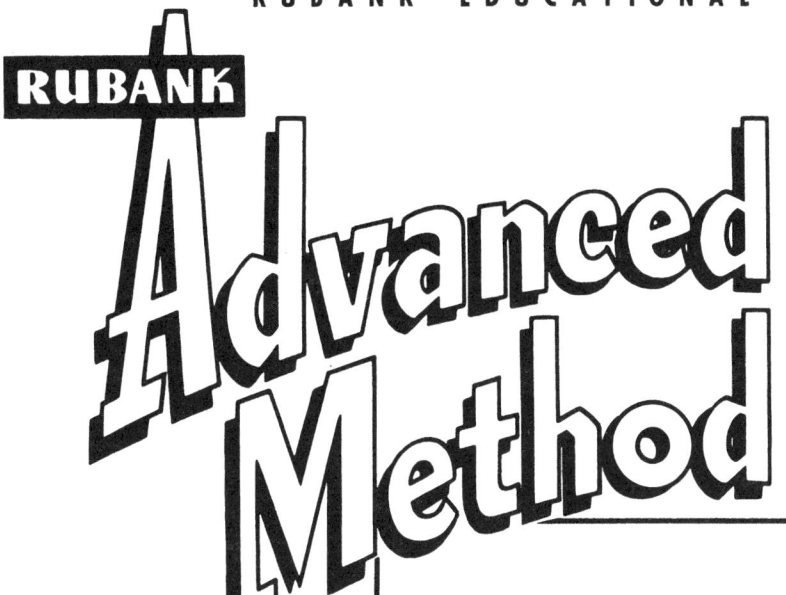

# TROMBONE OR BARITONE

## Vol. I

**WM. GOWER**
AND
**H. VOXMAN**

AN OUTLINED COURSE OF STUDY
DESIGNED TO FOLLOW UP ANY
OF THE VARIOUS ELEMENTARY
AND INTERMEDIATE METHODS

HAL•LEONARD® CORPORATION
7777 W. BLUEMOUND RD. P.O.BOX 13819 MILWAUKEE, WI 53213

# NOTE

**THE RUBANK ADVANCED METHOD** for Trombone or Baritone is published in two volumes, the course of study being divided in the following manner:

Vol. I { Keys of B♭, E♭, F, A♭, and C Major.
{ Keys of G, C, D, F, and A Minor.

Vol. II { Keys of D♭, G, G♭, D, C♭, and A Major.
{ Keys of B♭, E, E♭, and B Minor.

# PREFACE

**THIS METHOD** is designed to follow any of the various Elementary and Intermediate instruction series, or Elementary instruction series comprising two or more volumes, depending upon the previous development of the student. The authors have found it necessary in their teaching experience to draw from many sources in order to provide a progressive course of study. The present publication assembles in two volumes, the material essential to a well-rounded musical development.

**THE OUTLINES**, one of which is included in each of the respective volumes, tend to afford an objective picture of the student's progress. They will facilitate the ranking of members in a large ensemble or they may serve as a basis for awards of merit. In addition, a one-sided development along strictly technical or strictly melodic lines is avoided. The use of these outlines, however, is not imperative and they may be discarded at the discretion of the teacher.

*Wm. Gower — H. Voxman*

# Chromatic Chart for Trombone and Baritone

1. The B♮ or C♭ in the staff is too sharp. Flatten this tone enough to make it in good tune.
2. The C above the staff will be too flat. Shorten the position on the trombone enough to make it in tune. On the baritone the first and third valves may be used in slow passages to correct this pitch.
3. The D above the staff is sometimes too flat. Use first and second valves on baritone or fourth position on trombone to correct this.
4. The G above the staff in the second position on trombone must be made in short second (2-) to be in tune.
5. The F♯ or G♭ above the staff in the third position on trombone must be made in short third (3-).

## TABLE OF HARMONICS

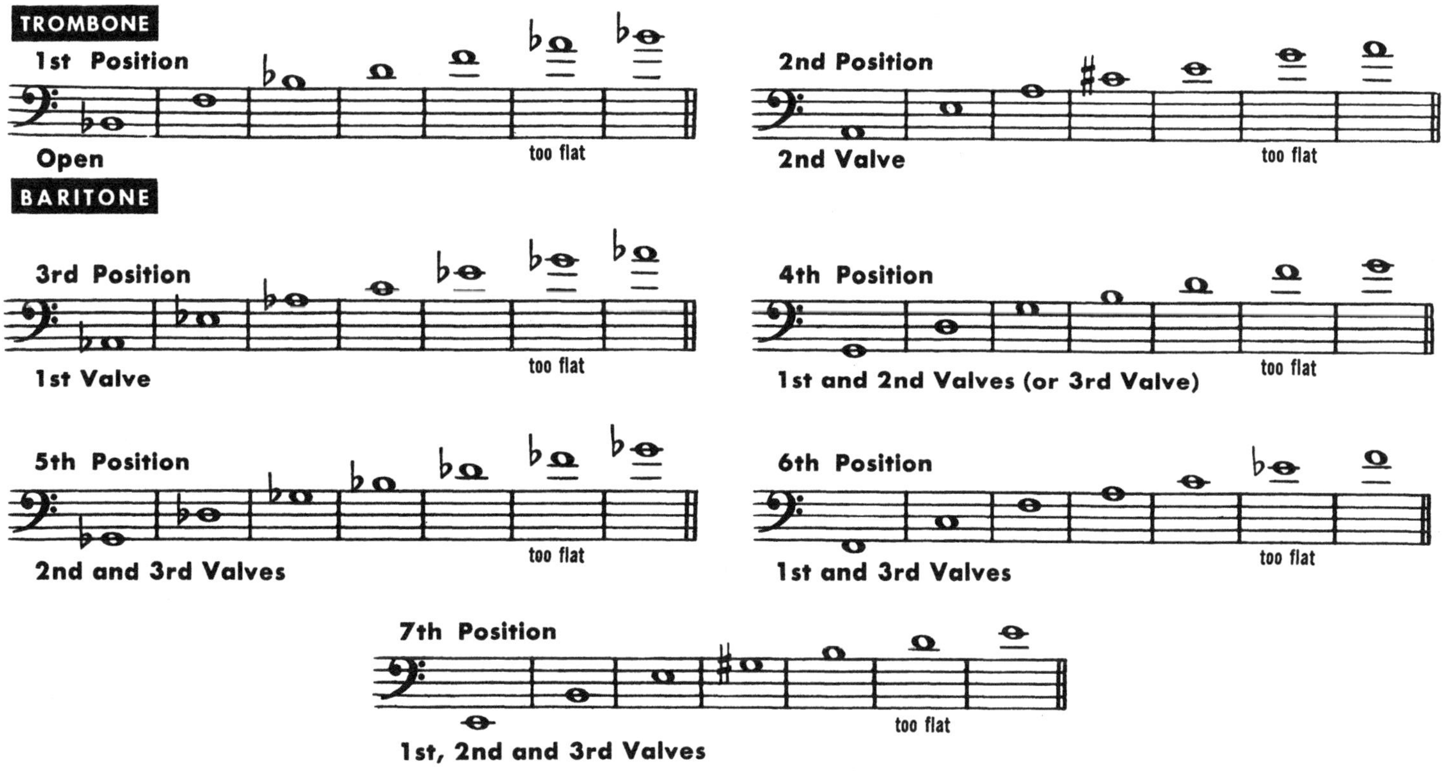

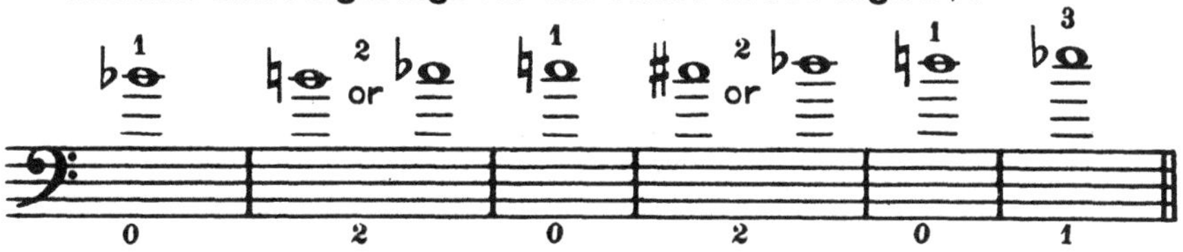

Copyright MCMXLI by Rubank, Inc. Chicago, Ill.
International Copyright Secured
Copyright Renewed

# OUTLINE OF RUBANK ADVANCED METHOD FOR TROMBONE, Vol. I

BY Wm. Gower and H. Voxman

| UNIT | SCALES and ARPEGGIOS | | | | (Key) | MELODIC INTERPRETATION | | ARTICULATION | | FLEXIBILITY EXERCISES | | MISCELLANEOUS PROBLEMS | | SOLOS | | UNIT COMPLETED |
|---|---|---|---|---|---|---|---|---|---|---|---|---|---|---|---|---|
| 1  | 7  | ① | 8 | ⑤ |    | B♭ | 19 | ① | 49 | ① | 60 | ① | 63 | ① | 70 | ① | |
| 2  | 7  | ② | 8 | ⑥ |    | B♭ | 19 | ② | 49 | ② | 60 | ① | 63 | ① | 70 | ① | |
| 3  | 7  | ③ | 8 | ⑦ |    | B♭ | 20 | ③ | 50 | ③ | 60 | ② | 63 | ② | 70 | ① | |
| 4  | 8  | ④ | 8 | ⑧ |    | B♭ | 21 | ④ | 50 | ④ | 60 | ② | 63 | ② | 70 | ① | |
| 5  | 8  | ⑨ |   |   |    | g  | 22 | ⑤ | 50 | ⑤ | 60 | ③ | 63 | ③ | 70 | ① | |
| 6  | 8  | ⑩ | 9 | ⑫ |    | g  | 22 | ⑥ | 51 | ⑥ | 60 | ③ | 63 | ③ | 70 | ① | |
| 7  | 9  | ⑪ |   |   |    | g  | 23 | ⑦ | 51 | ⑦ | 60 | ④ | 63 | ④ | 71 | ② | |
| 8  | 9  | ⑬ | ⑭ | ⑮ |   | g  | 23 | ⑦ | 51 | ⑦ | 60 | ④ | 63 | ④ | 71 | ② | |
| 9  | 10 | ⑯ | 11 | ⑳ |   | E♭ | 24 | ⑧ | 51 | ⑧ | 60 | ⑤ | 63 | ⑤ | 71 | ② | |
| 10 | 10 | ⑰ | 11 | ㉑ |   | E♭ | 25 | ⑨ | 52 | ⑨ | 60 | ⑤ | 63 | ⑤ | 71 | ② | |
| 11 | 10 | ⑱ | 11 | ㉒ |   | E♭ | 26 | ⑩ | 52 | ⑩ | 60 | ⑥ | 65 | ⑥ | 71 | ② | |
| 12 | 10 | ⑲ |   |   |    | E♭ | 26 | ⑩ | 52 | ⑩ | 60 | ⑥ | 65 | ⑦ | 71 | ② | |
| 13 | 11 | ㉓ | ㉕ |   |    | c  | 27 | ⑪ | 52 | ⑪ | 60 | ⑦ | 65 | ⑦ | 72 | ③ | |
| 14 | 11 | ㉔ |   |   |    | c  | 28 | ⑫ | 53 | ⑫ | 60 | ⑦ | 65 | ⑧ | 72 | ③ | |
| 15 | 11 | ㉖ | 12 | ㉗ | ㉘ | c  | 28 | ⑫ | 53 | ⑬ | 61 | ⑧ | 65 | ⑨ | 72 | ③ | |
| 16 | 12 | ㉙ | 13 | ㉝ |   | F  | 29 | ⑬ | 53 | ⑭ | 61 | ⑧ | 65 | ⑨ | 72 | ③ | |
| 17 | 12 | ㉚ | 13 | ㉞ |   | F  | 29 | ⑬ | 54 | ⑮ | 61 | ⑨ | 65 | ⑨ | 72 | ③ | |
| 18 | 12 | ㉛ | 13 | ㉟ |   | F  | 31 | ⑭ ⑮ | 54 | ⑮ | 61 | ⑨ | 66 | ⑩ | 72 | ③ | |
| 19 | 12 | ㉜ | 13 | ㊱ |   | F  | 32 | ⑯ | 54 | ⑯ | 61 | ⑨ | 66 | ⑩ | 73 | ④ | |
| 20 | 13 | ㊲ |   |   |    | d  | 33 | ⑰ | 54 | ⑰ | 61 | ⑩ | 66 | ⑩ | 73 | ④ | |
| 21 | 13 | ㊳ |   |   |    | d  | 34 | ⑱ | 55 | ⑱ | 61 | ⑩ | 66 | ⑮ | 73 | ④ | |
| 22 | 14 | ㊴ | ㊵ | ㊶ |   | d  | 34 | ⑱ | 55 | ⑲ | 61 | ⑩ | 66 | ⑮ | 73 | ④ | |
| 23 | 14 | ㊷ | 15 | ㊻ |   | A♭ | 35 | ⑲ | 55 | ⑳ | 62 | ⑪ | 67 | ⑯ | 73 | ④ | |
| 24 | 14 | ㊸ | 15 | ㊼ |   | A♭ | 35 | ⑲ | 56 | ㉑A | 62 | ⑪ | 67 | ⑯ | 73 | ④ | |
| 25 | 14 | ㊹ | 15 | ㊽ |   | A♭ | 38 | ⑳A | 57 | ㉒A | 62 | ⑫ | 67 | ⑰ | 74 | ⑤ | |
| 26 | 15 | ㊺ |   |   |    | A♭ | 38 | ⑳A | 57 | ㉒A | 62 | ⑫ | 67 | ⑰ | 74 | ⑤ | |
| 27 | 15 | ㊾ | 16 | 53 |   | f  | 39 | ㉑A | 57 | ㉓ | 62 | ⑬ | 67 | ⑱ | 74 | ⑤ | |
| 28 | 15 | 50 | 16 | 52 | 54 | f  | 40 | ㉒ | 57 | ㉔ | 62 | ⑬ | 67 | ⑱ | 74 | ⑤ | |
| 29 | 15 | 51 |   |   |    | f  | 40 | ㉒ | 57 | ㉔ | 62 | ⑭ | 68 | ㉓ | 74 | ⑤ | |
| 30 | 16 | 55 | 17 | 59 |   | C  | 41 | ㉓ | 58 | ㉕ | 62 | ⑭ | 68 | ㉓ | 74 | ⑤ | |
| 31 | 17 | 56 | 18 | 60 |   | C  | 41 | ㉓ | 58 | ㉖ | 62 | ⑮ | 68 | ㉔ | 75 | ⑥ | |
| 32 | 17 | 57 | 18 | 61 |   | C  | 43 | ㉔ | 58 | ㉗ | 62 | ⑮ | 68 | ㉕ | 75 | ⑥ | |
| 33 | 17 | 58 | 18 | 62 |   | C  | 43 | ㉔ | 58 | ㉗ | 62 | ⑮ | 69 | ㉖ | 75 | ⑥ | |
| 34 | 18 | 63 |   |   |    | a  | 46 | ㉕A | 59 | ㉘ | 62 | ⑮ | 69 | ㉖ | 75 | ⑥ | |
| 35 | 18 | 64 |   |   |    | a  | 47 | ㉖ | 59 | ㉙A | 62 | ⑯ | 69 | ㉗ | 75 | ⑥ | |
| 36 | 18 | 65 | 66 | 67 |   | a  | 48 | ㉗ | 59 | ㉙A | 62 | ⑯ | 69 | ㉗ | 75 | ⑥ | |

NUMERALS designate page number.
ENCIRCLED NUMERALS designate exercise number.
COMPLETED EXERCISES may be indicated by crossing out the rings, thus, ⊗.

# OUTLINE OF RUBANK ADVANCED METHOD FOR BARITONE, Vol. I
### BY Wm. Gower and H. Voxman

| UNIT | SCALES and ARPEGGIOS | | | | | (Key) | MELODIC INTERPRE-TATION | | ARTICU-LATION | | FLEXIBILITY EXERCISES | | ORNA-MENTS | | | SOLOS | | UNIT COMPLETED |
|---|---|---|---|---|---|---|---|---|---|---|---|---|---|---|---|---|---|---|
| 1 | 7 | (1) | 8 | (5) | | B♭ | 19 | (1) | 49 | (1) | 60 | (1) | 64 | (1) | | 70 | (1) | |
| 2 | 7 | (2) | 8 | (6) | | B♭ | 19 | (2) | 49 | (2) | 60 | (1) | 64 | (1) | | 70 | (1) | |
| 3 | 7 | (3) | 8 | (7) | | B♭ | 20 | (3) | 50 | (3) | 60 | (2) | 64 | (2) | | 70 | (1) | |
| 4 | 8 | (4) | 8 | (8) | | B♭ | 21 | (4) | 50 | (4) | 60 | (2) | 64 | (3) | | 70 | (1) | |
| 5 | 8 | (9) | | | | g | 22 | (5) | 50 | (5) | 60 | (3) | 64 | (4) | | 70 | (1) | |
| 6 | 8 | (10) | 9 | (12) | | g | 22 | (6) | 51 | (6) | 60 | (3) | 64 | (5) | | 70 | (1) | |
| 7 | 9 | (11) | | | | g | 23 | (7) | 51 | (7) | 60 | (4) | 65 | (6) | | 71 | (2) | |
| 8 | 9 | (13) | (14) | (15) | | g | 23 | (7) | 51 | (7) | 60 | (4) | 65 | (7) | | 71 | (2) | |
| 9 | 10 | (16) | 11 | (20) | | E♭ | 24 | (8) | 51 | (8) | 60 | (5) | 65 | (8) | | 71 | (2) | |
| 10 | 10 | (17) | 11 | (21) | | E♭ | 25 | (9) | 52 | (9) | 60 | (5) | 65 | (9) | | 71 | (2) | |
| 11 | 10 | (18) | 11 | (22) | | E♭ | 26 | (10) | 52 | (10) | 60 | (6) | 65 | (9) | | 71 | (2) | |
| 12 | 10 | (19) | | | | E♭ | 26 | (10) | 52 | (10) | 60 | (6) | 66 | (10) | | 71 | (2) | |
| 13 | 11 | (23) | (25) | | | c | 27 | (11) | 52 | (11) | 60 | (7) | 66 | (10) | | 72 | (3) | |
| 14 | 11 | (24) | | | | c | 28 | (12) | 53 | (12) | 60 | (7) | 66 | (11) | | 72 | (3) | |
| 15 | 11 | (26) | 12 | (27) | (28) | c | 28 | (12) | 53 | (13) | 61 | (8) | 66 | (12) | | 72 | (3) | |
| 16 | 12 | (29) | 13 | (33) | | F | 29 | (13) | 53 | (14) | 61 | (8) | 66 | (13) | | 72 | (3) | |
| 17 | 12 | (30) | 13 | (34) | | F | 29 | (13) | 54 | (15) | 61 | (9) | 66 | (14) | | 72 | (3) | |
| 18 | 12 | (31) | 13 | (35) | | F | 31 | (14) (15) | 54 | (15) | 61 | (9) | 66 | (15) | | 72 | (3) | |
| 19 | 12 | (32) | 13 | (36) | | F | 32 | (16) | 54 | (16) | 61 | (9) | 67 | (16) | | 73 | (4) | |
| 20 | 13 | (37) | | | | d | 33 | (17) | 54 | (17) | 61 | (10) | 67 | (17) | | 73 | (4) | |
| 21 | 13 | (38) | | | | d | 34 | (18) | 55 | (18) | 61 | (10) | 67 | (18) (19) | | 73 | (4) | |
| 22 | 14 | (39) | (40) | (41) | | d | 34 | (18) | 55 | (19) | 61 | (10) | 67 | (20) | | 73 | (4) | |
| 23 | 14 | (42) | 15 | (46) | | A♭ | 35 | (19) | 55 | (20) | 62 | (11) | 67 | (21) | | 73 | (4) | |
| 24 | 14 | (43) | 15 | (47) | | A♭ | 35 | (19) | 56 | (21) | 62 | (11) | 67 | (22) | | 73 | (4) | |
| 25 | 14 | (44) | 15 | (48) | | A♭ | 36 | (20) | 56 | (22) | 62 | (12) | 68 | (23) | | 74 | (5) | |
| 26 | 15 | (45) | | | | A♭ | 36 | (20) | 57 | (23) | 62 | (12) | 68 | (24) | | 74 | (5) | |
| 27 | 15 | (49) | 16 | (53) | | f | 38 | (21) | 57 | (24) | 62 | (13) | 68 | (25) | | 74 | (5) | |
| 28 | 15 | (50) | 16 | (52) | (54) | f | 40 | (22) | 57 | (24) | 62 | (13) | 69 | (26) | | 74 | (5) | |
| 29 | 15 | (51) | | | | f | 40 | (22) | 58 | (25) | 62 | (14) | 69 | (26) | | 74 | (5) | |
| 30 | 16 | (55) | 17 | (59) | | C | 41 | (23) | 58 | (26) | 62 | (14) | 69 | (27) | | 74 | (5) | |
| 31 | 17 | (56) | 18 | (60) | | C | 41 | (23) | 58 | (27) | 62 | (15) | 69 | (27) | | 75 | (6) | |
| 32 | 17 | (57) | 18 | (61) | | C | 43 | (24) | 58 | (27) | 62 | (15) | 69 | (28) | | 75 | (6) | |
| 33 | 17 | (58) | 18 | (62) | | C | 43 | (24) | 58 | (27) | 62 | (15) | 69 | (29) | | 75 | (6) | |
| 34 | 18 | (63) | | | | a | 45 | (25) | 59 | (28) | 62 | (15) | 69 | (30) | | 75 | (6) | |
| 35 | 18 | (64) | | | | a | 47 | (26) | 59 | (29) | 62 | (16) | 69 | (31) | | 75 | (6) | |
| 36 | 18 | (65) | (66) | (67) | | a | 47 | (26) | 59 | (29) | 62 | (16) | 69 | (32) | | 75 | (6) | |

NUMERALS designate page number.
ENCIRCLED NUMERALS designate exercise number.
COMPLETED EXERCISES may be indicated by crossing out the rings, thus,

# PRACTICE AND GRADE REPORT

## SECOND SEMESTER

Student's Name _____  Date _____

| Week | Sun. | Mon. | Tue. | Wed. | Thu. | Fri. | Sat. | Total | Parent's Signature | Grade |
|------|------|------|------|------|------|------|------|-------|--------------------|-------|
| 1    |      |      |      |      |      |      |      |       |                    |       |
| 2    |      |      |      |      |      |      |      |       |                    |       |
| 3    |      |      |      |      |      |      |      |       |                    |       |
| 4    |      |      |      |      |      |      |      |       |                    |       |
| 5    |      |      |      |      |      |      |      |       |                    |       |
| 6    |      |      |      |      |      |      |      |       |                    |       |
| 7    |      |      |      |      |      |      |      |       |                    |       |
| 8    |      |      |      |      |      |      |      |       |                    |       |
| 9    |      |      |      |      |      |      |      |       |                    |       |
| 10   |      |      |      |      |      |      |      |       |                    |       |
| 11   |      |      |      |      |      |      |      |       |                    |       |
| 12   |      |      |      |      |      |      |      |       |                    |       |
| 13   |      |      |      |      |      |      |      |       |                    |       |
| 14   |      |      |      |      |      |      |      |       |                    |       |
| 15   |      |      |      |      |      |      |      |       |                    |       |
| 16   |      |      |      |      |      |      |      |       |                    |       |
| 17   |      |      |      |      |      |      |      |       |                    |       |
| 18   |      |      |      |      |      |      |      |       |                    |       |
| 19   |      |      |      |      |      |      |      |       |                    |       |
| 20   |      |      |      |      |      |      |      |       |                    |       |

Semester Grade _____

Instructor's Signature _____

## FIRST SEMESTER

Student's Name _____  Date _____

| Week | Sun. | Mon. | Tue. | Wed. | Thu. | Fri. | Sat. | Total | Parent's Signature | Grade |
|------|------|------|------|------|------|------|------|-------|--------------------|-------|
| 1    |      |      |      |      |      |      |      |       |                    |       |
| 2    |      |      |      |      |      |      |      |       |                    |       |
| 3    |      |      |      |      |      |      |      |       |                    |       |
| 4    |      |      |      |      |      |      |      |       |                    |       |
| 5    |      |      |      |      |      |      |      |       |                    |       |
| 6    |      |      |      |      |      |      |      |       |                    |       |
| 7    |      |      |      |      |      |      |      |       |                    |       |
| 8    |      |      |      |      |      |      |      |       |                    |       |
| 9    |      |      |      |      |      |      |      |       |                    |       |
| 10   |      |      |      |      |      |      |      |       |                    |       |
| 11   |      |      |      |      |      |      |      |       |                    |       |
| 12   |      |      |      |      |      |      |      |       |                    |       |
| 13   |      |      |      |      |      |      |      |       |                    |       |
| 14   |      |      |      |      |      |      |      |       |                    |       |
| 15   |      |      |      |      |      |      |      |       |                    |       |
| 16   |      |      |      |      |      |      |      |       |                    |       |
| 17   |      |      |      |      |      |      |      |       |                    |       |
| 18   |      |      |      |      |      |      |      |       |                    |       |
| 19   |      |      |      |      |      |      |      |       |                    |       |
| 20   |      |      |      |      |      |      |      |       |                    |       |

Semester Grade _____

Instructor's Signature _____

# Scales and Arpeggios
## B♭ Major

* Numbers above notes indicate trombone positions.

4

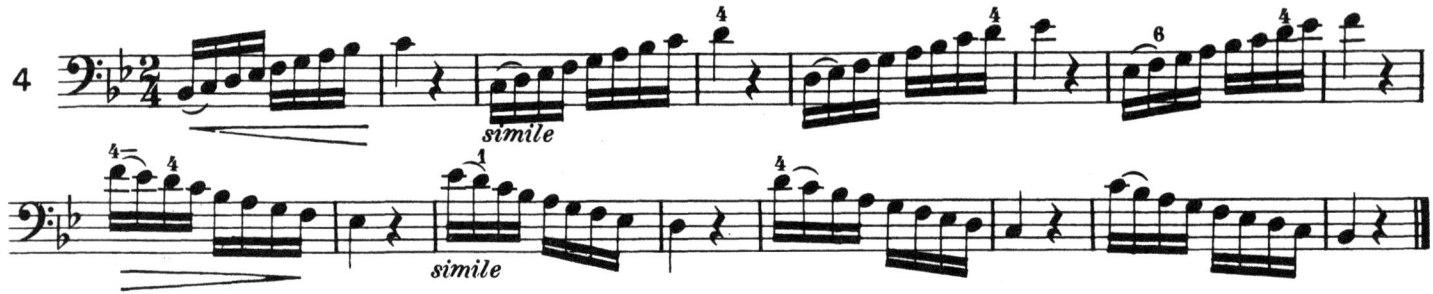

Various articulations may be used in the chromatic, the interval, and the chord studies at the instructor's option.

Chromatic Scale

5

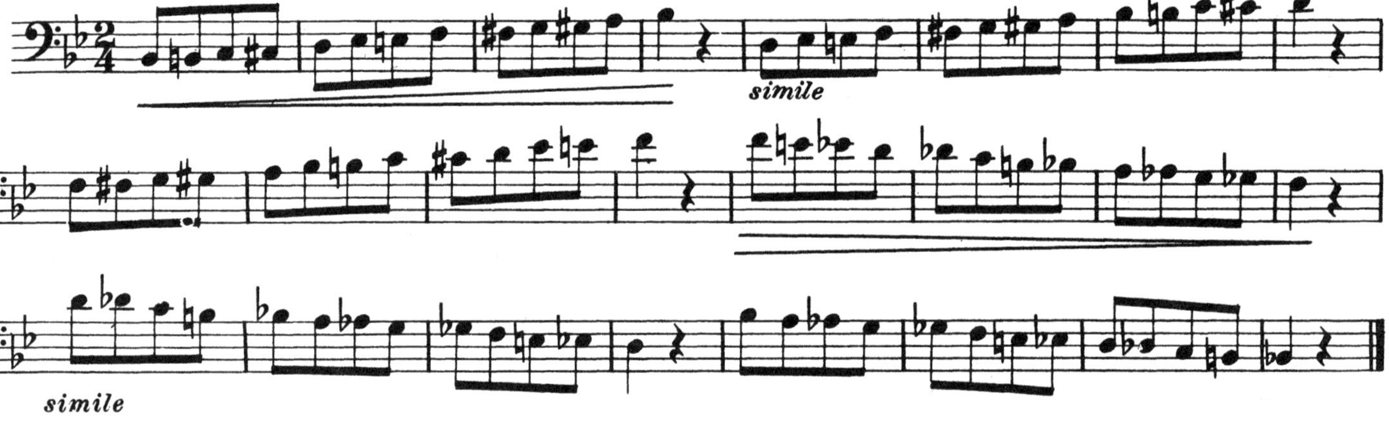


Exercise in Thirds

6

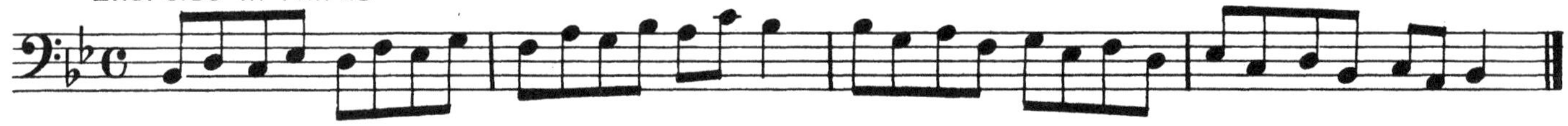

Common Chord

7

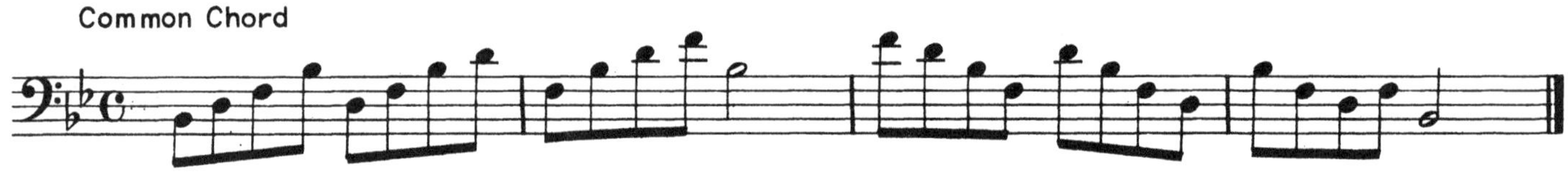

Dominant 7th Chord

8

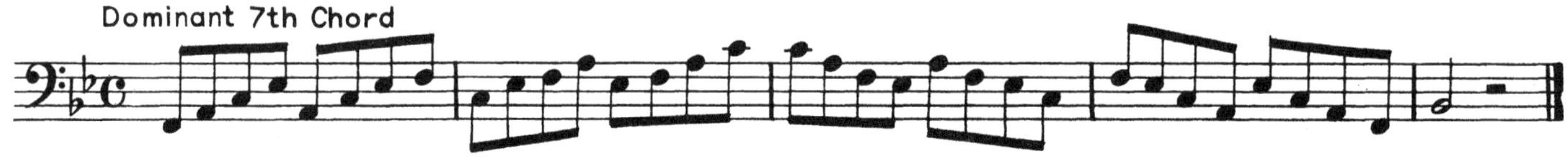

## G Minor

The sign ^ indicates a half-step

Natural — Harmonic

9

Melodic

10

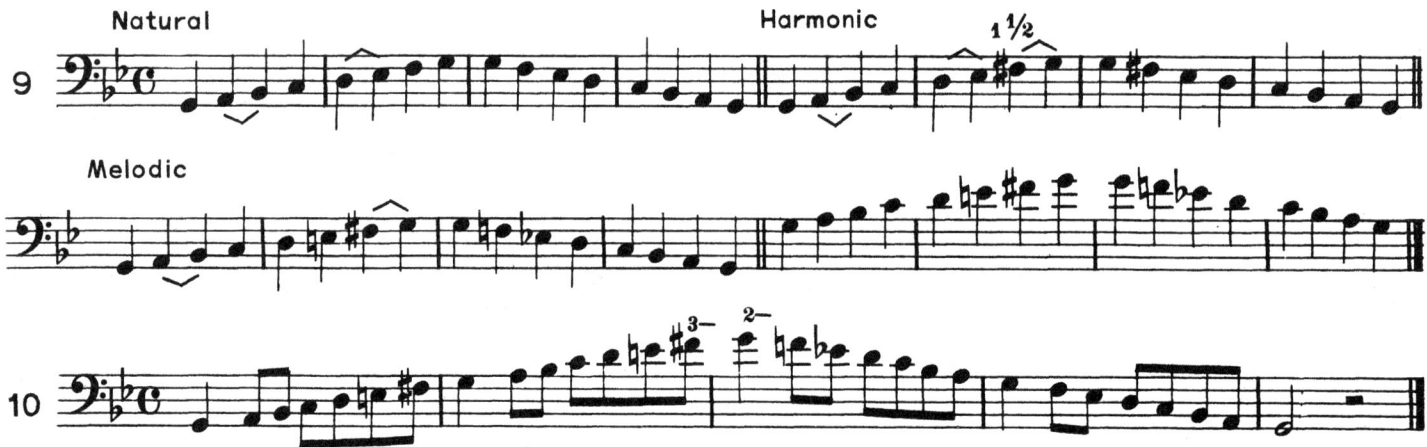

# E♭ Major

# Studies in Melodic Interpretation

## For One or Two Part Playing

The following studies are designed to aid in the development of the student's interpretative ability. Careful attention to the marks of expression is essential to effective use of the material. Pencil the technically difficult passages and devote extra time to their mastery.

In rhythmic music in the more rapid tempi (marches, dances, etc.), tones that are equal divisions of the beat are played somewhat detached (staccato). Tones that equal a beat or are multiples of a beat are held full value. Tones followed by rests are usually held full value. The latter should be especially observed in slow music as well.

BORTNIANSKY

Moderato

1

HOHMANN

Allegro

2

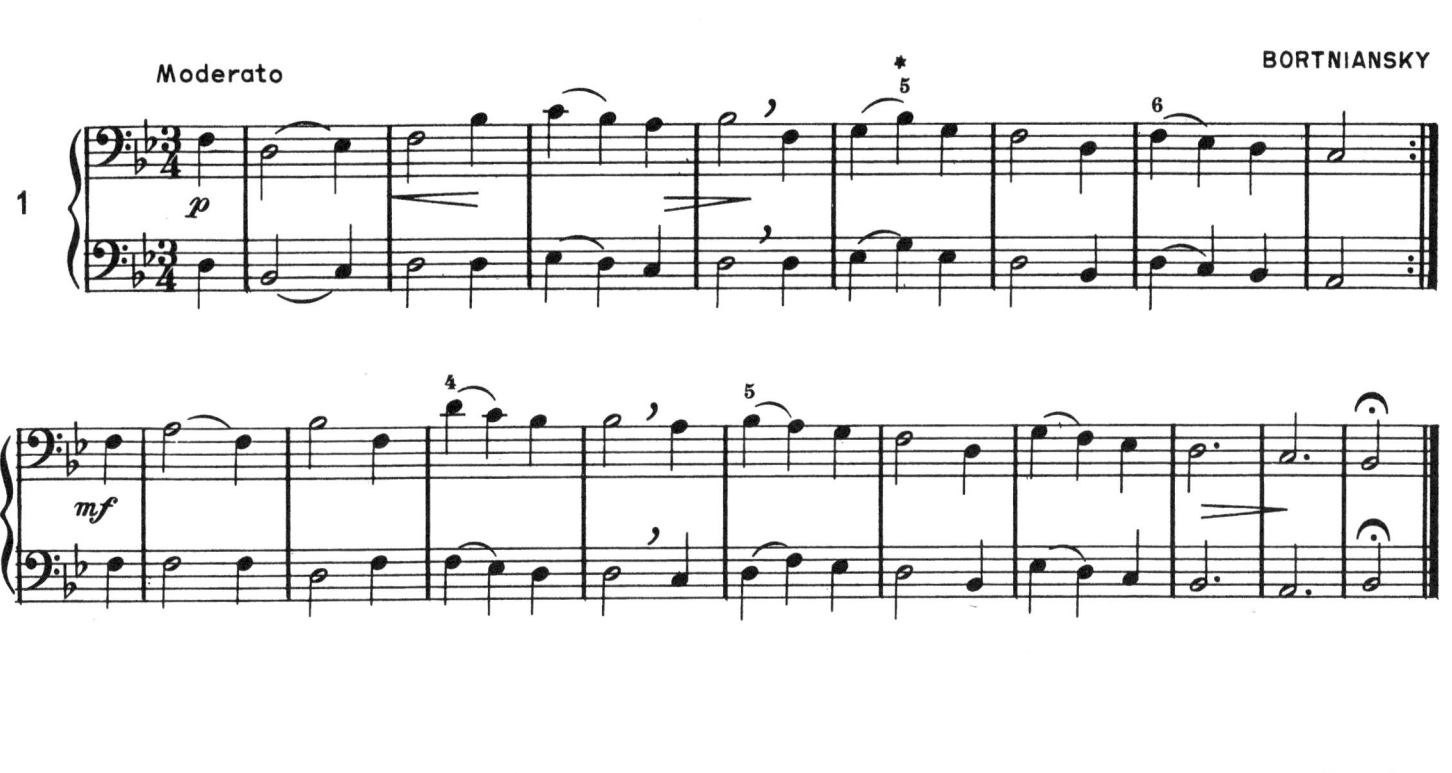

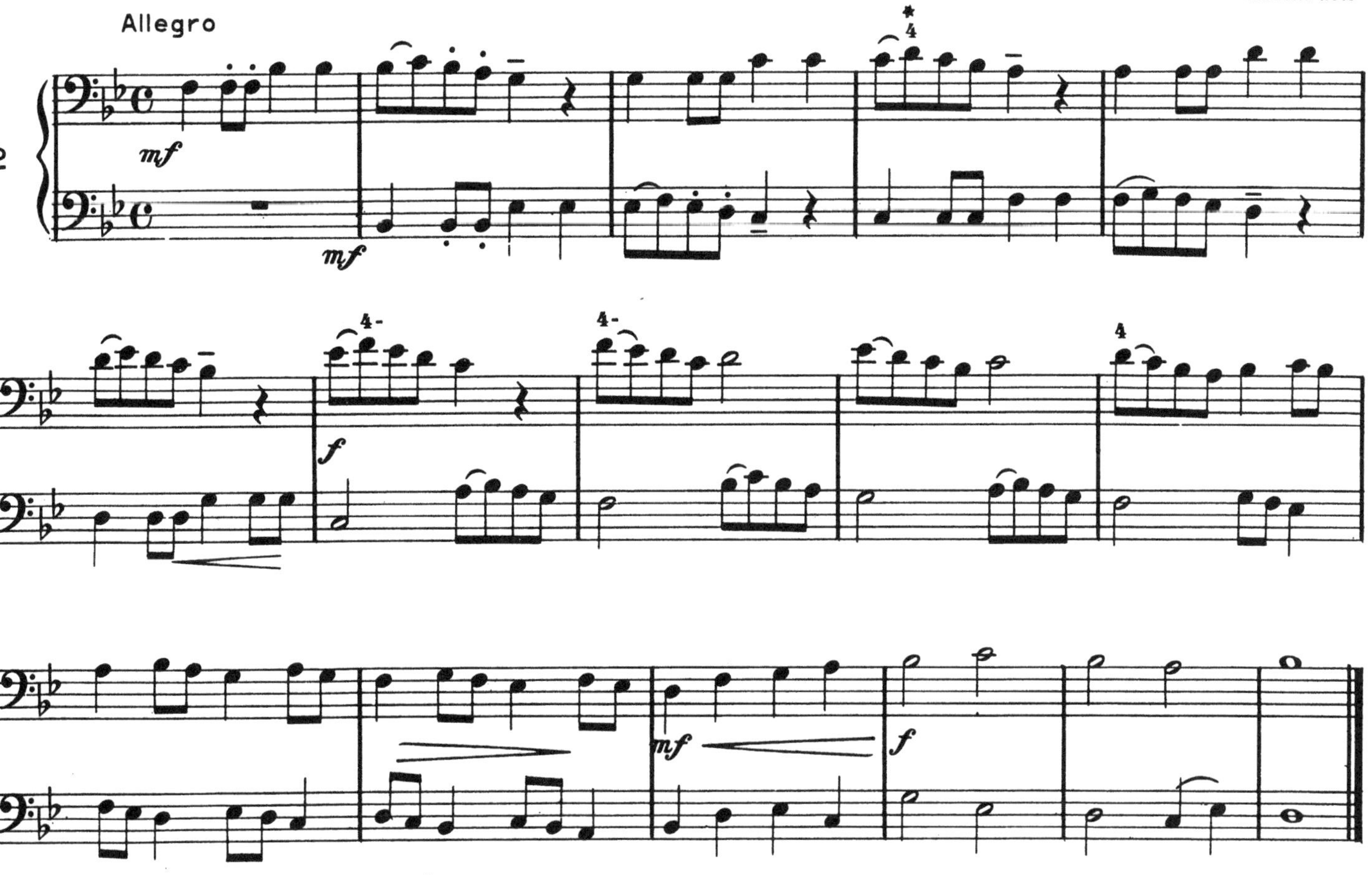


* Numbers above notes indicate trombone positions.

\* _trattenuto = ritardando_

24

SELTNER

8 Moderato

Moderato

SAINT-JACOME

9

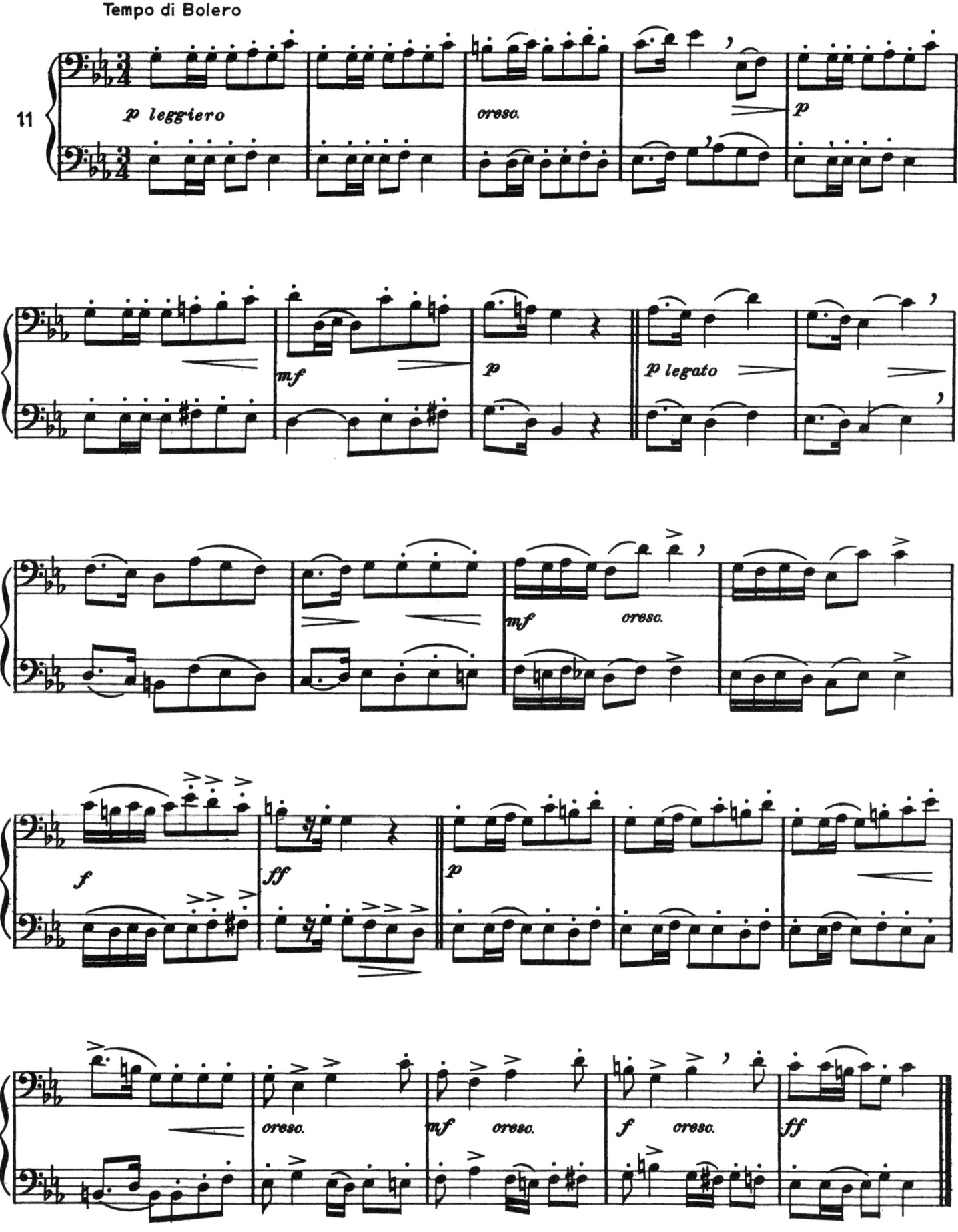

27

De GOUY

Tempo di Bolero

Andantino grazioso

13

*p dolce*

BONNISSEAU

\* stentando = retarding the tempo

Play all detached eighth notes in this exercise somewhat staccato.

SAINT-JACOME

* Baritones only.

CARNAUD

** Trombones only.
* Baritones only.

**21 A** Andantino — CORNETTE

** Trombones only.

22

BONNISSEAU

GATTI

23

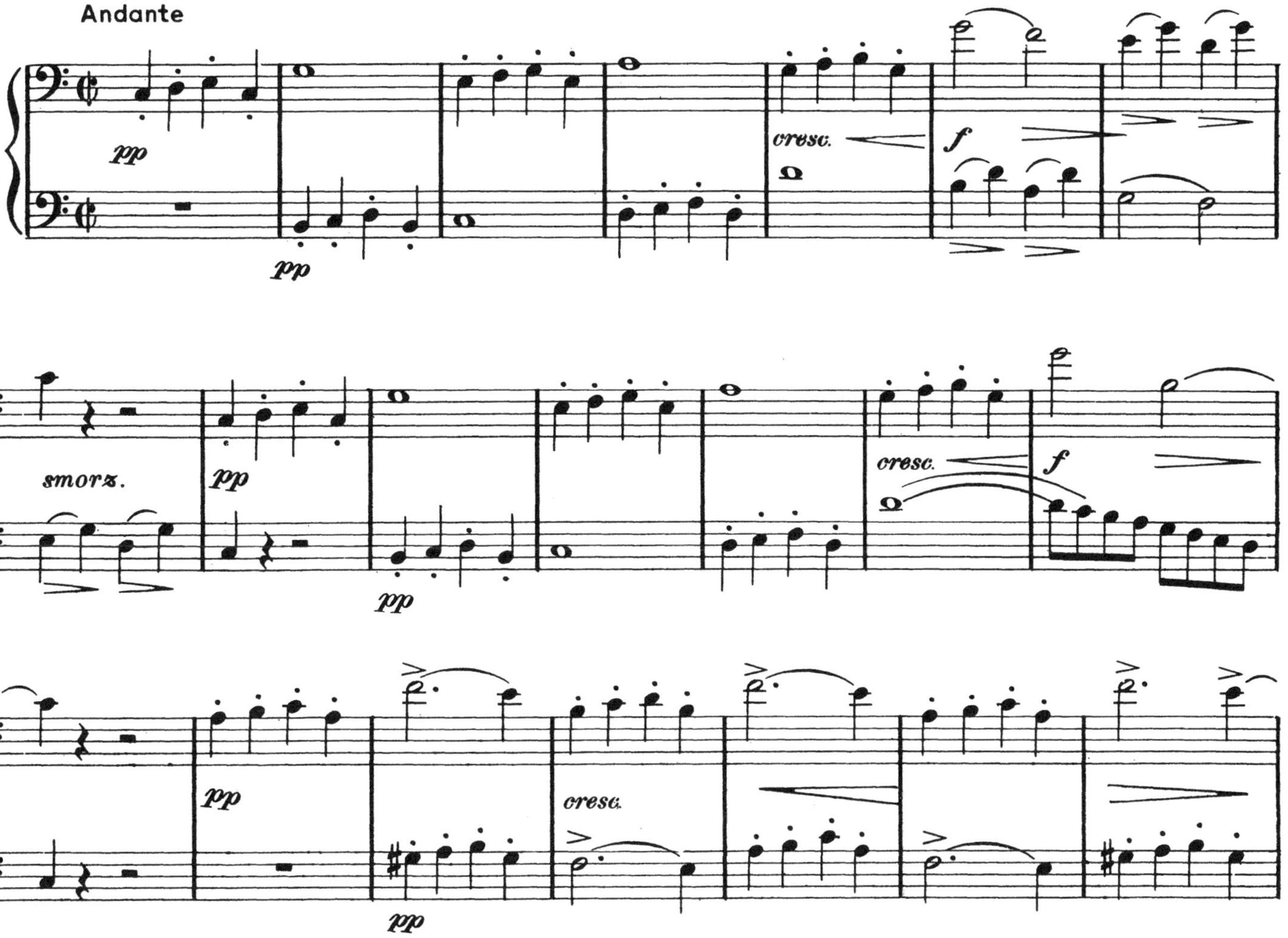

Andante sostenuto  De GOUY

* Baritones only.

** Trombones only.

47

CORNETTE

48

Allegro

BÖHM

27

** Trombones only.

# Studies in Articulation

In all exercises where no tempo is indicated the student should play the study as rapidly as is consistent with tonal control and technical accuracy. The first practice on each exercise should be done very slowly in order that the articulation may be carefully observed.

In allegro tempi figures similar to  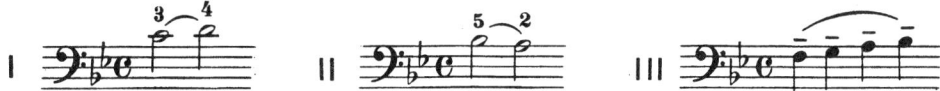 should be performed  etc. The figure  should be played.

The slur is a difficult articulation on the slide trombone. Whenever possible the motion of the slide should be outward when playing an ascending slurred passage (Ex.I) and inward when playing a descending slurred passage (Ex.II).

When it is not possible to move the slide as recommended above, the tones under the slur should be tongued as lightly as possible, fully sustained, and free of any trace of glissando. See Ex.III.

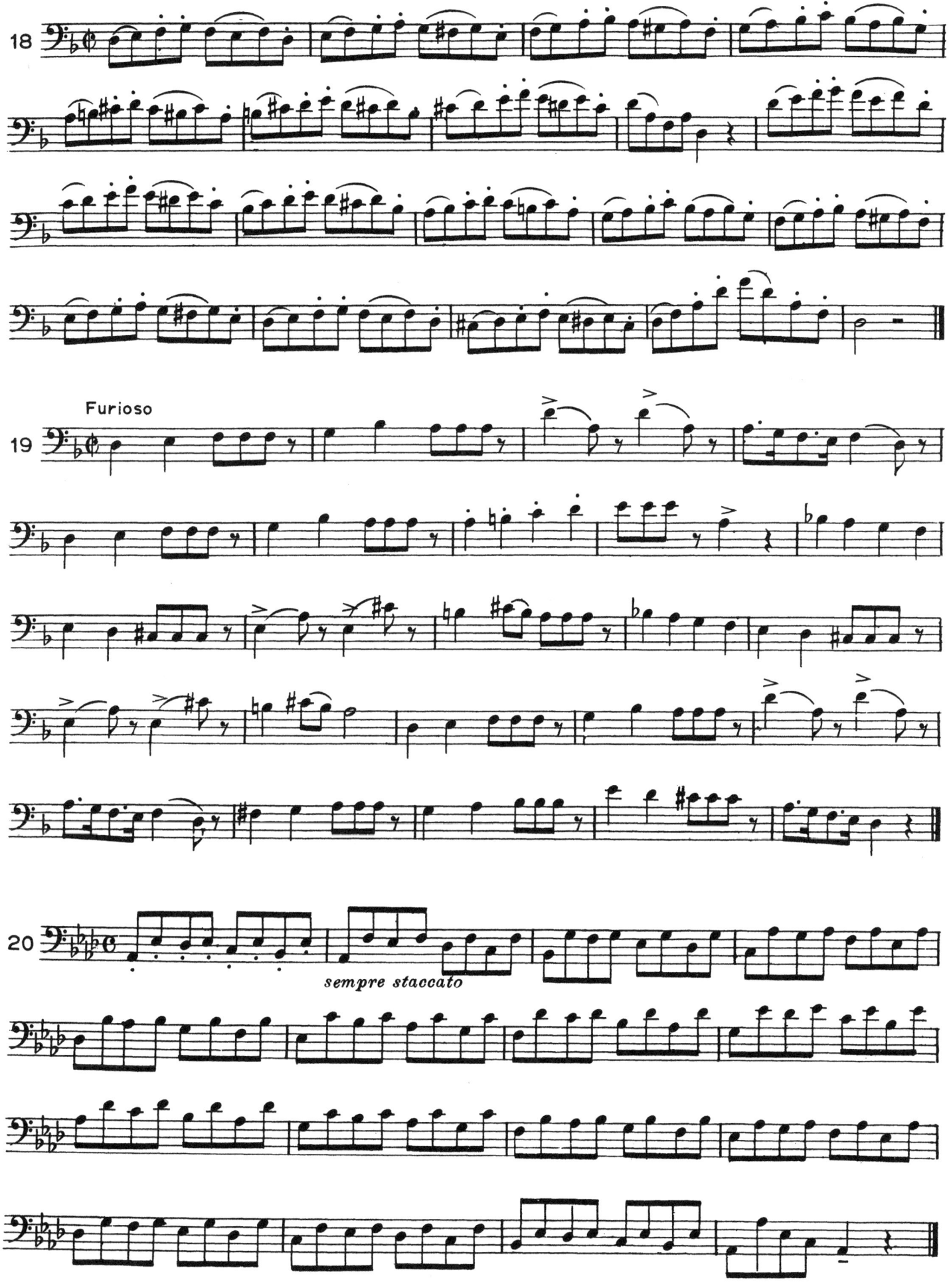

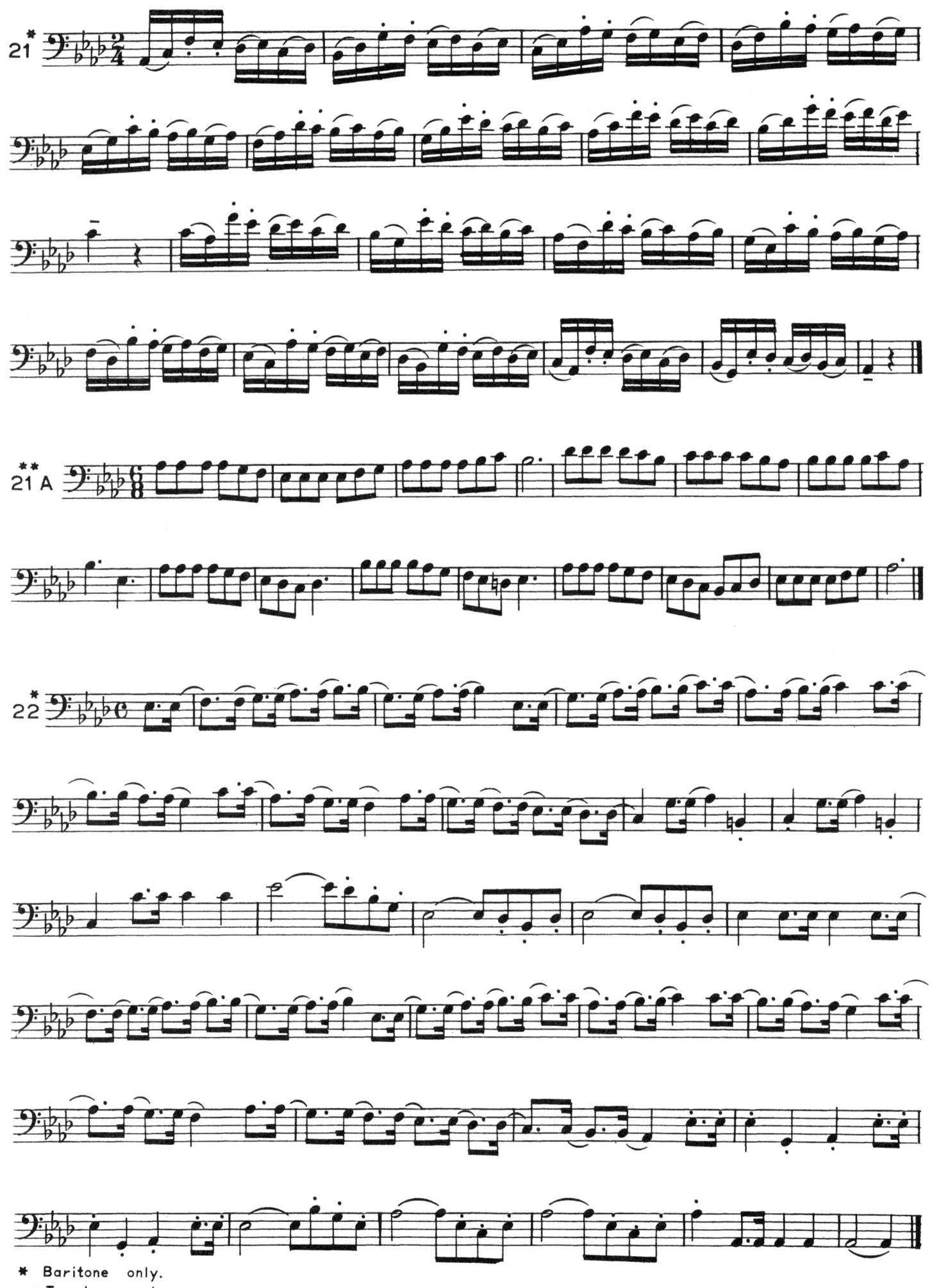

* Baritone only.
** Trombone only.

** Trombone only.

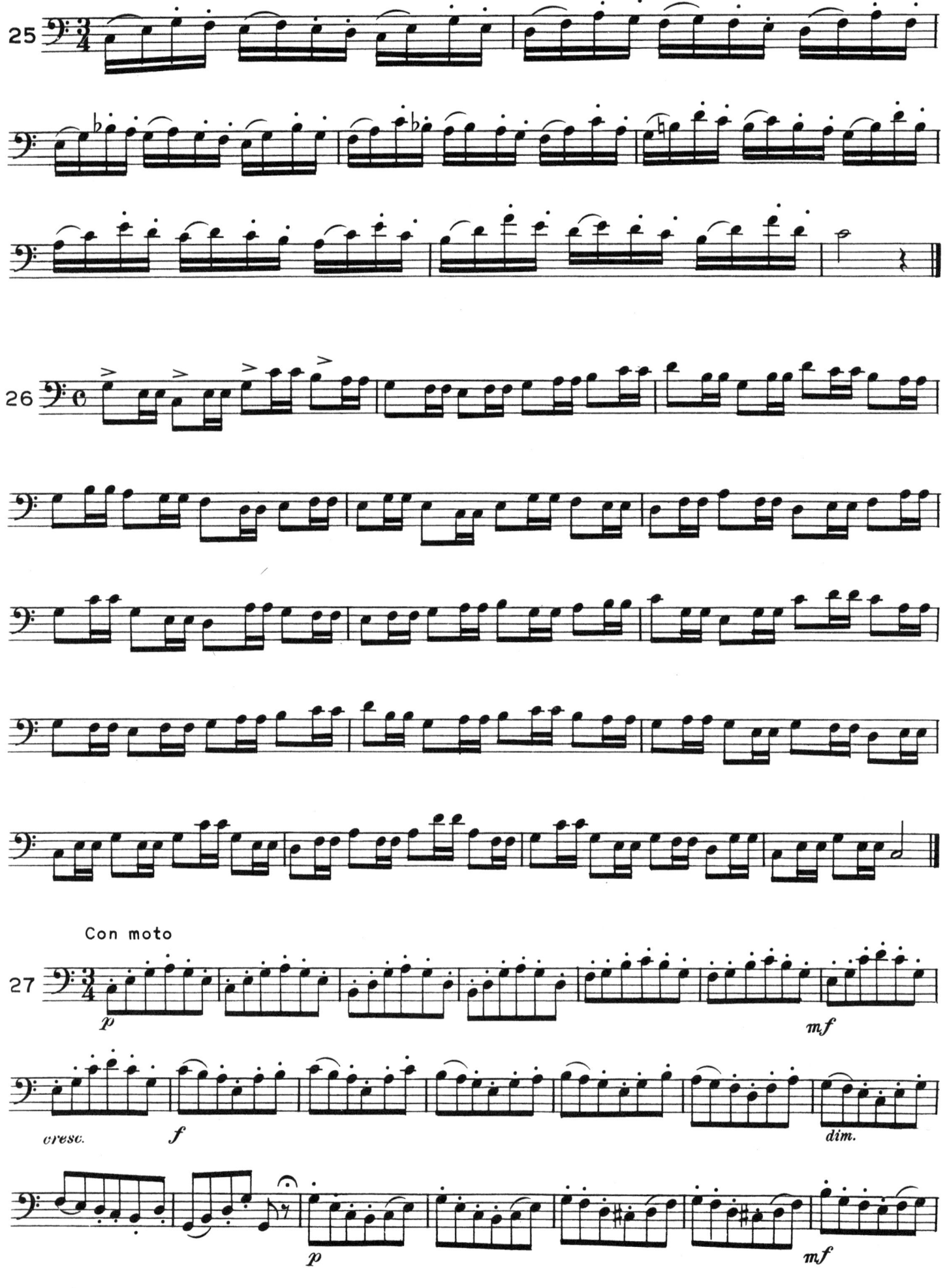

* Baritone only.
** Trombone only.

# Flexibility Exercises

Keep the tone well sustained throughout the slur indicated, leaving no gaps between the tones. The slur must be made smoothly and evenly by the flexibility of the embouchure.

Adhere strictly to the fingerings given. Trombone positions will be indicated above the notes.

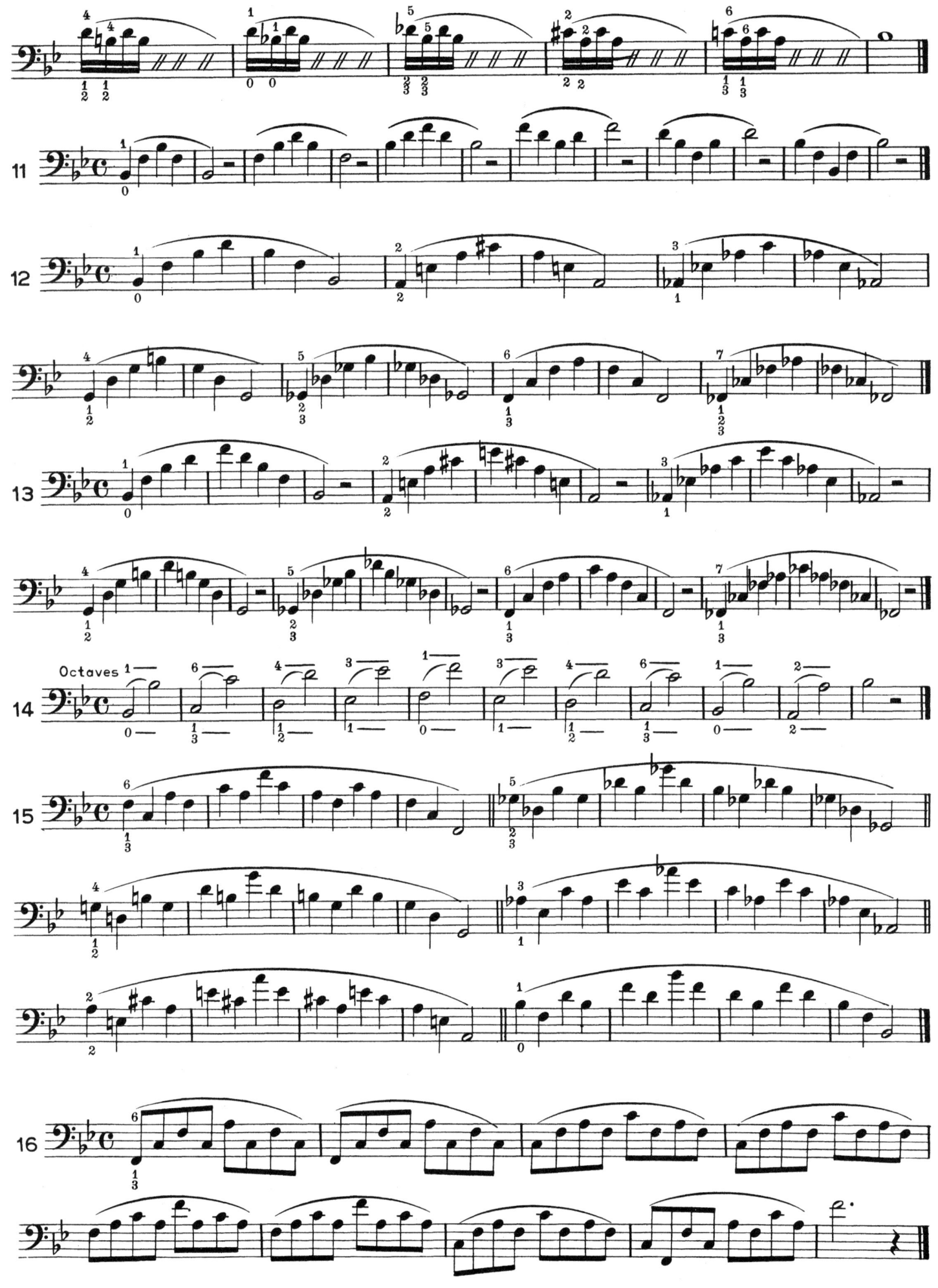

# Position Studies for Trombone**

The studies in this section have a two-fold purpose; first, to familiarize the student with the different positions in which these tones may be played, and second, to establish an accurate memory for the correct length of these positions.

Care must be taken to maintain the same quality of tone in playing a note in its various positions.

These exercises should be practiced daily until mastered and must then be memorized.

** Trombone only.

# Musical Ornamentation (Embellishments)

The following treatment of ornamentation is by no means complete. It is presented here only as a guide to the execution of those ornaments which the student may encounter at this stage of his musical development. There are different manners of performing the same ornament.

The execution of certain ornaments is not feasible on the slide trombone, for example, the trill. However, from the standpoint of the students' musical development, it is desirable that he be familiar with their interpretation. Refer to the trombone outline for exercises to be studied.

## The Trill (Shake)

The trill (or shake) consists of the rapid alternation of two tones. They are represented by the printed note (called the principal note) and the next tone above in the diatonic scale. The interval between the two tones may be either a half-step or a whole-step. The signs for the trill are 𝑡𝑟 and ∿.

An accidental when used in conjunction with the trill sign affects the upper note of the trill.

\* Baritone only.

# Grace Notes (Appoggiatura)

The grace notes are indicated by notes of a smaller size. They may be divided into two classes: long and short.

from "Serenade" Haydn

In instrumental music of recent composition the short grace notes should occupy as little time as possible and that value is taken preceding the principal note. They may be single, double, triple or quadruple, as the case may be. The single short grace note is printed as a small eighth note with a stroke through its hook. It is not to be accented. Use trill fingerings when fundamental fingerings are too difficult.

ARBAN

10
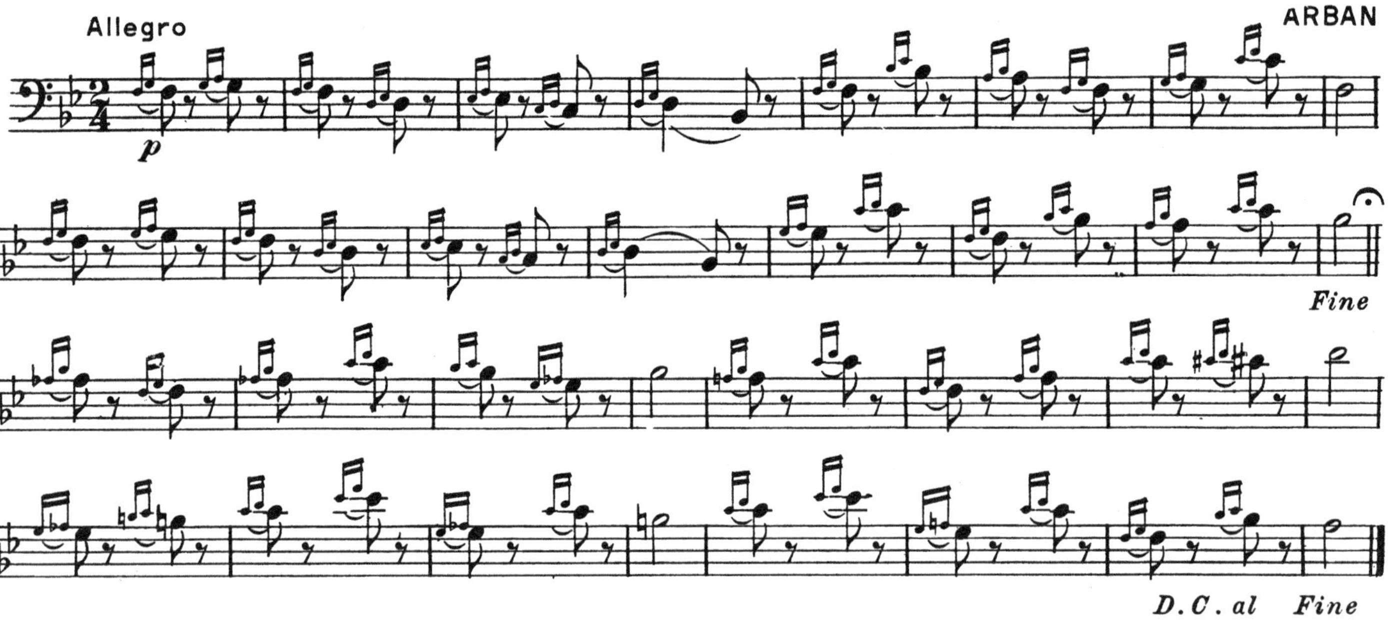


11*
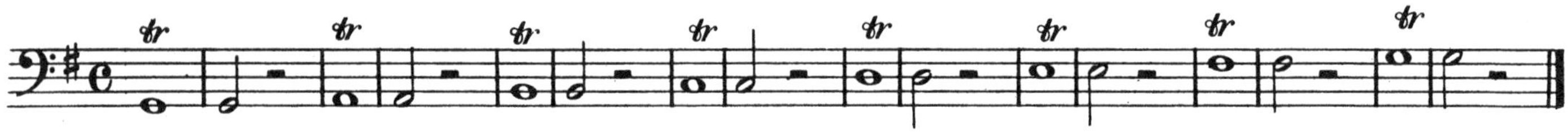

12*
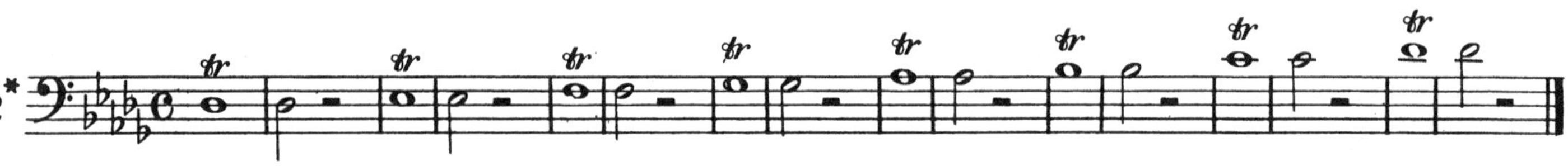

13*
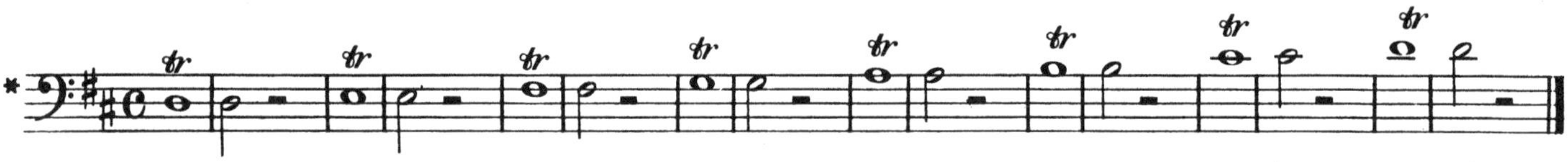

14*
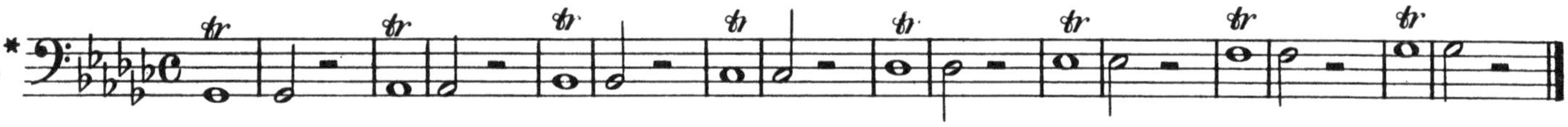

## The Mordent

The short mordent (⩚) consists of a single rapid alternation of the principal note with its lower auxiliary. Two or more alternations are executed in the long mordent.

The inverted mordent (𝆗) does not have the cross line. In it the lower auxiliary is replaced by the upper. It is the more commonly used mordent in music for the wind instruments.

The mordent takes its value from the principal note.

15


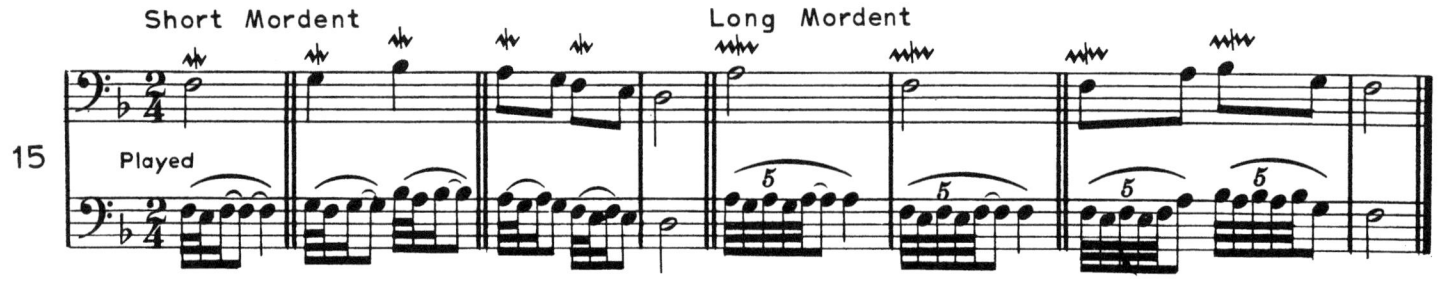

* Baritone only.

Short inverted mordent Long inverted mordent

16 


Allegretto moderato ARBAN

17 


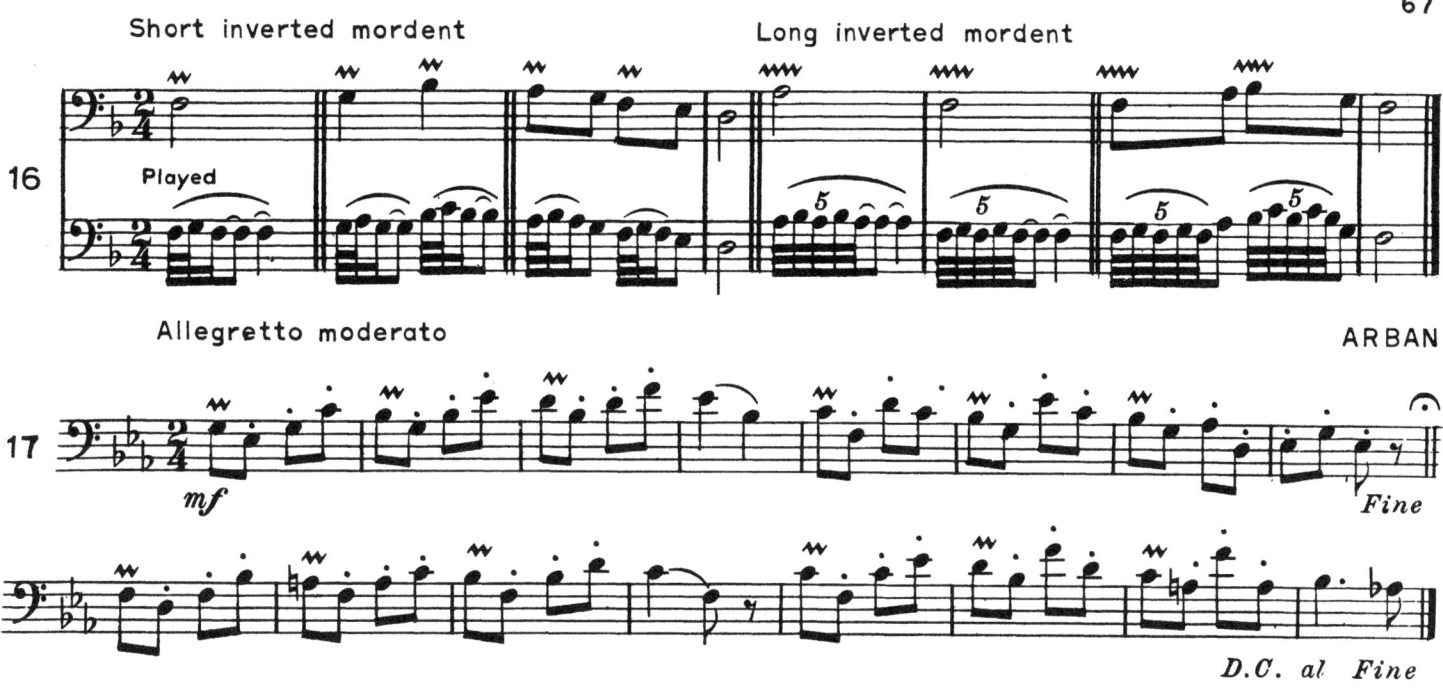

In trills of sufficient length a special ending is generally used whether indicated or not 


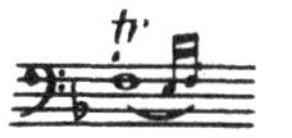

The closing of the trill consists of two tones: the scale tone below the principal note and the principal note.

In long trills of a solo character, it is good taste to commence slowly and gradually increase the speed. Practice the following exercises in the manner of both examples 1 and 2.

Ex. 1 Ex. 2

18 


19* 

20* 

21* 

22* 

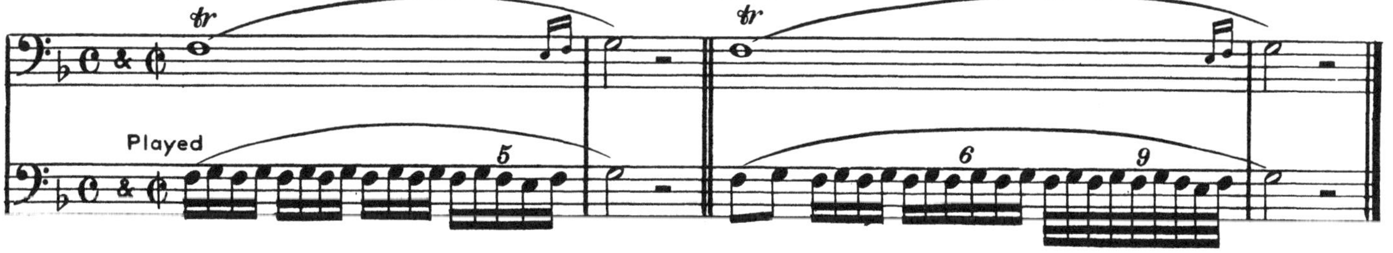

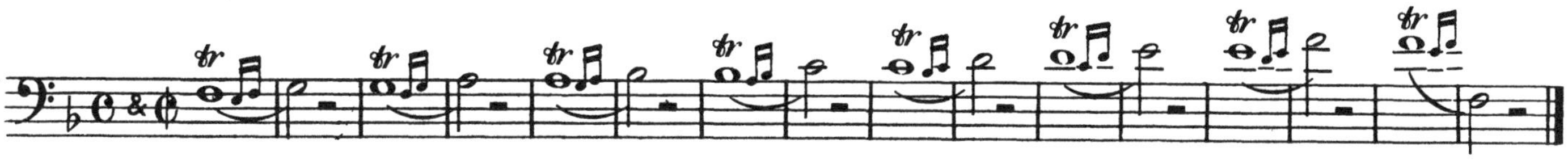

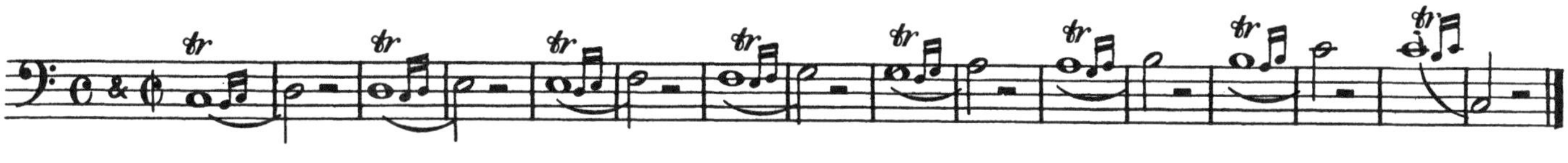

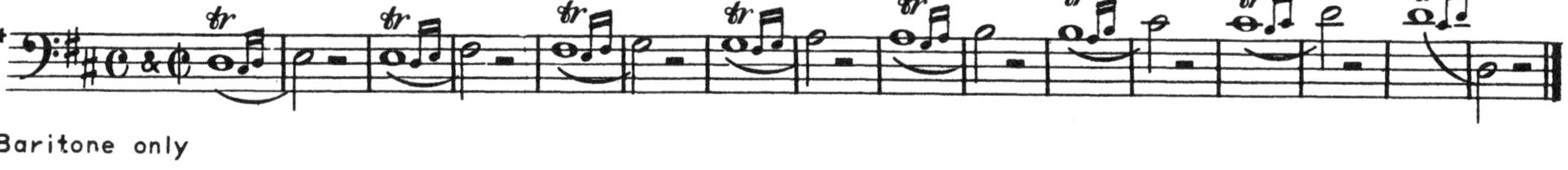

* Baritone only

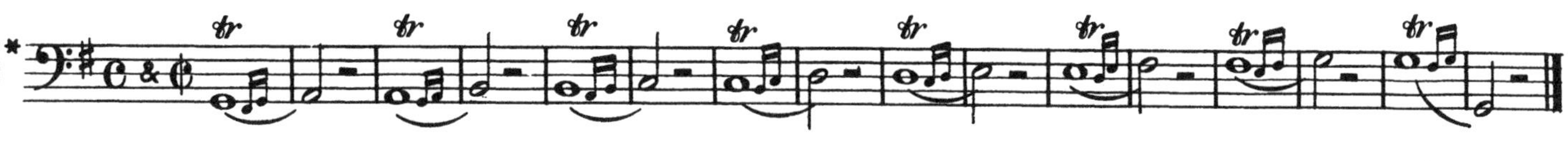

# The Turn (Gruppetto)

The turn consists of four tones: the next scale tone above the principal tone, the principal tone itself, the tone below the principal tone, and the principal tone again.

When the turn ∞ is placed to the right of the note, the principal tone is held almost to its full value, then the turn is played just before the next melody tone. In this case (Ex. 1, 2, 3, 4 and 5) the four tones are of equal length.

When the turn is placed between a dotted note and another note having the same value as the dot (Ex. 6 and 8), the turn is then played with the last note of the turn taking the place of the dot, making two notes of the same value. The turn sign after a dotted note will indicate that one melody note lies hidden in the dot.

Sometimes an accidental sign occurs with the turn, and in this case when written below the sign, it refers to the lowest tone of the turn, but when written above, to the highest. (Ex. 1 & 2 below).

When the turn is placed over a note (Ex. 3) the tones are usually played quickly, and the fourth tone is then held until the time value of the note has expired.

In the inverted turn (Ex. 4) the order of tones is reversed, the lowest one coming first, the principal next, the highest third and the principal tone again, last. The inverted turn is indicated by the ordinary turn sign reversed: ∾ or by ⁊.

* Baritone only.

# SOLOS

# CROSS AND CROWN

Solo Trombone or Baritone

CARLETON L. COLBY

# Calm As the Night

Solo Trombone or Baritone

C. BOHM

# FRIENDS
## WALTZ CAPRICE

Solo Trombone or Baritone

CLAY SMITH

# Cantique de Noel

**Solo Trombone** or Baritone

ADOLPHE ADAM
Transcribed by G.E. Holmes

# Awakening of Spring

Romance

Solo Trombone or Baritone

E. BACH

# Berceuse

Solo Trombone 𝄢 or Baritone

OSKAR BÖHME, Op. 7

# PRINCIPAL TERMS USED IN MUSIC

|  |  |
|---|---|
| A | To, in, or at; a tempo, in time. |
| Accelerando (accel.) | Gradually increasing the speed. |
| Accent | Emphasis on certain parts of the measure. |
| Adagio | Slowly; leisurely. |
| Ad libitum (ad lib.) | At pleasure; not in strict time. |
| A due (a 2) | To be played by both instruments. |
| Affettuoso | With feeling. |
| Agitato | Restless, with agitation. |
| All or Alla | In the style of. |
| Alla Marcia | In the style of a March. |
| Allegretto | Diminutive of allegro; moderately fast, lively; faster than andante; slower than allegro. |
| Allegro (All°) | Lively; brisk; rapid. |
| Allegro assai | Very rapidly. |
| Amoroso | Affectionately. |
| Andante | A slow movement; moderately slow. |
| Andantino | Diminutive of andante; strictly, slower than andante, but often used in the reverse sense. |
| Anima, con / Animato | With animation. |
| A piacere | At pleasure; equivalent to ad libitum. |
| Appassionato (Appass.) | Impassioned. |
| Arpeggio | A broken chord. |
| Assai | Very; Allegro assai, very rapidly. |
| A tempo | In the original tempo. |
| Attacca | Attack or begin what follows without pausing. |
| Ben | Well; rather. |
| Bis | Twice; repeat the passage. |
| Brillante | Showy; sparkling; brilliant. |
| Brio, con | With much spirit. |
| Cadenza (cad.) | An elaborate florid passage introduced as an embellishment. |
| Cantabile | In a singing style. |
| Capriccio a | At pleasure; ad libitum. |
| Coda | A supplement at the end of a composition. |
| Col or con | With. |
| Con fuoco | With fire. |
| Crescendo (cresc.) | Swelling; increasing in loudness. |
| Da or dal | From. |
| Da Capo (D. C.) | From the beginning. |
| Dal Signo (D. S.) | From the sign. |
| Decrescendo (decresc.) | Decreasing in strength. |
| Diminuendo (dim.) | Gradually softer. |
| Divisi (div.) | Divided, each part to be played by a separate instrument. |
| Dolce (dol.) | Softly; sweetly. |
| Dolcissimo | Very sweetly and softly. |
| Duet or Duo | A composition for two performers. |
| E | And. |
| Elegante | Elegant; graceful. |
| Energico | With energy; vigorously. |
| Enharmonic | Alike in pitch, but different in notation. |
| Espressivo (Espress.) | With expression. |
| Fine | The end. |
| Forte (f) | Loud. |
| Forte-piano (fp) | Accent strongly, diminishing instantly to piano. |
| Fortissimo (ff) | Very loud. |
| Forzando (fz >) | Indicates that a note or chord is to be strongly accented. |
| Forza | Force of tone. |
| Giocoso | Joyously; playfully. |
| Giusto | Exact; in strict time. |
| Grandioso | Grand; pompous; majestic. |
| Grave | Very slow and solemn. |
| Grazioso | Gracefully. |
| Key note | The first degree of the scale, the tonic. |
| Largamente | Very broad in style. |
| Larghetto | Slow, but not so slow as Largo; nearly like Andantino. |
| Largo | Broad and slow; the slowest tempo-mark. |
| Ledger-line | A small added line above or below the staff. |
| Legato | Smoothly; the reverse of staccato. |
| Leggiero | Lightly. |
| Lento | Slow, between Andante and Largo. |
| L'istesso tempo | In the same time (or tempo). |
| Loco | In place; play as written, no longer an octave higher or lower. |
| Ma | But. |
| Ma non troppo | But not too much so. |
| Maestoso | Majestically; dignified. |
| Maggiore | Major Key. |
| Marcato | Marked. |
| Meno | Less. |
| Meno mosso | Less quickly. |
| Mezzo | Half; moderately. |
| Mezzo-piano (mp) | Moderately soft. |
| Minore | Minor Key. |
| Moderato | Moderately. Allegro moderato, moderately fast. |
| Molto | Much; very. |
| Morendo | Dying away. |
| Mosso | Equivalent to rapid. Piu mosso, quicker. |
| Non | Not. |
| Notation | The art of representing musical sounds by means of written characters. |
| Obbligato | An indispensable part. |
| Opus (Op.) | A work. |
| Ossia | Or; or else. Generally indicating an easier method |
| Ottava (8va) | To be played an octave higher. |
| Pause (⌒) | The sign indicating a pause or rest. |
| Perdendosi | Dying away gradually. |
| Piacere, a | At pleasure. |
| Pianissimo (pp) | Very softly. |
| Piano (p) | Softly. |
| Piu | More. |
| Piu Allegro | More quickly. |
| Poco or un poco | A little. |
| Poco a poco | Gradually; by degrees; little by little. |
| Poco piu mosso | A little faster. |
| Poco meno | A little slower. |
| Poco piu | A little faster. |
| Pomposo | Pompous; grand. |
| Prestissimo | As quickly as possible. |
| Presto | Very quick; faster than Allegro. |
| Primo (1mo) | The first. |
| Quasi | As if; in the style of. |
| Rallentando (rall.) | Gradually slower. |
| Replica | Repetition. Senza replica, without repeats. |
| Rinforzando (rfz.) | With special emphasis. |
| Ritardando (rit.) | Gradually slower and slower. |
| Risoluto | Resolutely; bold; energetic. |
| Ritenuto | In slower time—not *gradually* slower. |
| Scherzando | Playfully; sportively. |
| Segue | Follow on; in similar style. |
| Semplice | Simply; unaffectedly. |
| Senza | Without. Senza sordino, without mute. |
| Sforzando (sf.) | Forcibly; with sudden emphasis. |
| Simile | In like manner. |
| Smorzando (smorz.) | Diminishing in sound. Equivalent to Morendo. |
| Solo | For one performer only. Soli, for all. |
| Sostenuto | Sustained; prolonged. |
| Sotto | Below; under. Sotto voce, in a subdued tone. |
| Spirito | Spirit. Con Spirito with spirit. |
| Staccato | Detached; separate. |
| Stentando | Dragging or retarding the tempo. |
| Stretto or stretta | An increase of speed. Piu stretto, faster. |
| Stringendo | Gradually faster. |
| Tacet | "Is silent." Signifies that an instrument or vocal part, so marked, is omitted during the movement or number in question. |
| Tempo | Movement; rate of speed. |
| Tempo primo | Return to the original tempo. |
| Tenuto (ten.) | Held for the full value. |
| Tonic | The key-note of any scale. |
| Tranquillo | Quietly. |
| Tremolando, Tremolo | A tremulous fluctuation of tone. |
| Trio | A piece of music for three performers. |
| Triplet | A group of three notes to be performed in the time of two of equal value in the regular rhythm. |
| Troppo | Too; too much. Allegro, ma non troppo, not too quickly. |
| Tutti | All; all the instruments. |
| Un | A; one; an. |
| Variatione | The transformation of a melody by means of harmonic, rhythmic and melodic changes and embellishments. |
| Veloce | Quick; rapid; swift. |
| Vivace | With vivacity; bright; spirited. |
| Vivo | Lively; spirited. |
| Volti Subito (V. S.) | Turn over quickly. |